It's ...... the mind, you know!

PHIL HUGHES

To Mum, who gave me so much love and a wonderful start in life.
Gone from this world you may be, but - as you did in life - you will live in my heart, always.

"If the only thing people learned was not to be afraid of their experience, that alone would change the world."

SYDNEY BANKS

"Thought is not reality; yet it is through Thought that our realities are created.
It is what we as humans put into our thoughts, that dictates what we think of life."

SYDNEY BANKS, The Missing Link

CONTENTS

FOREWORD BY AMY JOHNSON, Ph.D

This is a book of metaphors. But you probably know that already.

The thing about metaphors is that they aren't the important part. The metaphors themselves aren't the headliner. They are more like a really good prop that draws your eye left; they expand your vision and open you to seeing the entire scene with more depth.

That was a metaphor, by the way.

Metaphors are a collection of familiar words that point toward something important. The metaphors themselves are just words and images. The understanding to which they point is what it's all about.

So why not just talk directly about what these metaphors are pointing to?

We try. But as it turns out, the Principles behind all of life that Phil shares in this book are indescribable. It's like trying to verbally describe a sunset—words will never do it justice. It must be personally experienced in order to be known in any meaningful way.

These Principles that describe how life works aren't graspable with the intellect. Intellect actually tends to get in the way. Luckily, metaphors are like a Quaalude for your intellect, numbing it with familiar words and images so that a far bigger, deeper truth has room to emerge.

(It seems I literally cannot write this foreword without metaphors).

The Principles of Mind, Thought, and Consciousness are vast, spiritual and deep. They show us that we are all one. All that exists is one eternal, formless energy taking on an infinite number of temporary forms.

From these Principles we see that we are mentally and emotionally well by nature. That we live within the moment-to-moment creative energy of Thought, brought to life within us by Consciousness.

Everything we can see is impermanent and constantly in flux. This understanding leads us toward what lies beyond the world of our senses and beyond our psychology. There is a stable, unchanging "there" to which these metaphors point.

It's a peaceful and wise backdrop, before our thoughts,

feelings, identities and problems. In that space, all is well. In that space is everything practical and wise that can help us see our way through anything that shows up in our lives.

The understanding that will surface as you relax and explore this book has changed my own life in countless ways, big and small. It has done the same for Phil and for many, many people around the world.

It is commonly said that when people initially begin learning about these Principles, some of the metaphors they hear from others begin to resonate as truth. Watch for that as you read.

And it's said that as people really begin to feel grounded in these Principles, they naturally begin coming up with their own metaphors. This is where Phil is. He lives this understanding and so he sees it everywhere.

I've been blessed to be on this journey with Phil for several years now and I'm thrilled that he is sharing his insights in this way. He has a way of describing the indescribable that I know will help you see things in a new way.

Amy Johnson, Ph.D.
Author of *Being Human* and *The Little Book of Big Change: The No-Willpower Approach to Breaking Any Habit*

INTRODUCTION

WHY READ THIS BOOK?

In late 2011 I was idly browsing Amazon for a golf psychology book, when I came across the book *Stillpower* by Garret Kramer.

I read the blurb and was intrigued – a new paradigm, eh?

Many a psychology book had dusted my book shelves over the previous two decades, and while some helped for a while, none had a permanent impact. Like fireworks, many of the tips and techniques initially produced brilliant illumination, but all too soon the effects would fizzle and fade.

As with most people, I wanted the silver bullet, the sure-fire technique that I could go to in times of need and get the sure-fire result.

So as I read the first few pages of Stillpower, it rather surprised me that Garret advised the reader not to take notes, but to let the message soak into the sub-conscious and find whatever course it was going to.

Here was an author telling me I already had everything I needed to be successful and happy. It was just that much of it had been covered over by years of education and thinking.

What did I need to do to uncover these things that were naturally mine?

Nothing.

Nothing?

According to Garret, there was nothing to do but stay in the game, and let things unfold naturally, that all our experiences are created by thoughts, not circumstances.

Really?

It all seemed counterintuitive. The how-to books I'd been immersed in offered detailed instructions and step-by-step plans for achieving a specific result.

I was kind of surprised that while intellectually I resisted the message, I found myself experiencing a lovely feeling of warmth and peace.

There was one line in the book which particularly struck a

chord:

"Are your thoughts clear, are your feelings good, are you open to life's bigger picture?"

I loved the idea - your feelings are the barometer of your state of mind, so before acting, ask yourself how you are feeling. If you are feeling good, go ahead and act, if you aren't, don't.

I wasted no time turning that into a mantra. Dozens of times a day I would ask myself this question before acting.

The question helped, but not always.

I had missed the point. I had turned the question into a technique, a strategy for well-being.

I didn't understand that Stillpower was not about not acting, but recognizing the true source of your experience. It's not necessary to fix errant thoughts and feelings because they will automatically change when left alone.

While I thought "I had it", in truth I had no more than an intellectual understanding of what Garret was pointing to.

A deeper recognition of the paradigm's true meaning did not come until several months afterward. In the intervening weeks, many an insight would hit me from nowhere, but I still believed in my head that high performance was the result of carefully cultivating the right set of circumstances.

Then one day I was attending a Leadership Training course laid on by the company I worked for.

At the time, I was living in Texas, which tends to be a little bit warm most of the year. Although it was October, the temperature was still in the 80s, so I did not bother to pack a sweater for the short trip from Houston to Galveston.

This proved to be a mistake. While we were only just past that time of year when you can wander around with a marshmallow on a skewer and have it toasted in seconds, inside it was freezing cold. Texans tend to take pride in the ferocity of their air conditioning. Worse, there were limited clothing store options open at the times of day when I wasn't in training.

The one night I did go out clothes shopping, it was pouring with rain and by the time I arrived at the stores, they were shut. I was wet, miserable, and blaming my mood and inability to concentrate on malicious fate and the lack of a sweater, which would, of course, have changed my entire outlook into one of warm, comfortable focus.

By the morning of the last day, I had developed a bad head cold.

I awoke that morning feeling congested, thick-headed and sorry for myself, and clarity of thought was about as close to me as equatorial Africa is to the North Pole.

I had been re-reading *Stillpower* and had the thought,

"Just go with it. You're feeling bad. So what? Don't fight it. Just show up to the sessions, and whatever happens, happens."

I immediately started to feel better, less burdened by the need to be a certain way, to perform, or to bear down.

That morning the group split into two, with each looking at a different leadership topic. The subject of ours was "Resistance to Change in your Organization."

Group leader Linda was a master at inventing activities which drummed home her message far better than a thousand words ever could. She had us pair off, then told us the rules of the game.

There would be five rounds. In each round, we would turn our backs to our partners and perform a number of changes to our physical appearance. Then we would turn around and try to figure out what changes our partners had made. In the next round, we would make further changes, and so on. We were also told we could neither repeat changes, nor begin putting ourselves back together until Linda told us to.

In the first round, we had to make five changes in thirty seconds. I turned my glasses upside down, took off a shoe, undid a couple of buttons on my shirt, rolled up a trouser leg and took off my watch.

In each succeeding round, we had to make even more

changes with less time to do it.

By the last round, we had to make ten changes in twenty seconds.

By that time, it was difficult to know what to do. Most everyone had given up on the changes. It was too hard. Some, myself included, had started getting dressed again before Linda had said we could.

Which was exactly the point of the game - change can be hard, and people are resistant to it because it conflicts with how they think the world should be.

I loved the game. Gone were thoughts of how low and miserable I was. When Linda asked for one of us to report back to the other group on what we'd been doing, I had no hesitation in raising my hand.

For the next forty minutes, I sat and listened as our group shared stories. If I had thoughts about what was going on, I was not aware of them. I was completely immersed and enjoying how things were playing out. Story boards were created to help provide me with structure during the report out session.

As I sat in the report out session awaiting my turn, I had given little thought to what I would say. I was just calm, relaxed, with a feeling that I would know what to say and do when the time came.

When it did, I instinctively removed a shoe and undid a

few shirt buttons as I ambled to the front. This immediately had a few people laughing and I sensed they were intrigued by this unusual beginning.

As I began to talk, I made further changes, but didn't go too far with the undressing because of the fierce air conditioning. I still was not thinking about what to say, it was just flowing through me. I recounted a particularly inspiring story told by one of the facilitators. When it came to the story boards, I summarized all four without glancing at any of them. I had total recall. It was amazing, and felt so easy.

My talk was very well received. More than one delegate described it as their course highlight, while others said they wished they could present like me.
As I reflected on the day the thought occurred,

"That shouldn't have been possible. You felt terrible, and shouldn't have been able to perform."

Yet I did.

The further thought occurred that there was more in what Garret had shared than I had seen.

Wanting to build on what I had already learned, I started reading any book on this understanding that I could lay my hands on. I attended some excellent trainings. All of this led me to a much deeper appreciation of what was first shared with the world by a Scotsman named Sydney Banks.

The history of Sydney Banks and his epiphany have been covered at length by some brilliant practitioners, and I refer to these works in the bibliography at the back of this book.

But just to summarize:

An uneducated welder living in Canada, Syd had a sudden enlightenment experience in 1973 in which he realized that "there is no such thing as insecurity, only thought" and that everything in life originated from the same formless energy. From that moment until his death in 2009, he shared what he had learnt with thousands of people from all over the world.

He saw the simplicity in life - that rather than being humans in search of a spiritual experience, we are spiritual beings having a human experience, and that every human experience was being created from three building blocks, which he called Mind, Consciousness and Thought.

These building blocks are spiritual in nature and formless. Although they cannot be seen, their effects can, much in the way you cannot see gravity, but can witness its effects when dropping a pen.

Syd described them as:

Mind

Mind is the energy behind everything, whether it has form or not, the infinitely creative power behind life, the foundation for all existence. It has no beginning, and no end.

Consciousness

Consciousness enables us to be aware of all that is going on around us - situations, surroundings, events, people, our thoughts.

Thought

We interpret life via Thought. Every feeling, perception and experience we ever have, comes to us via the power of Thought.

Syd saw that if any one of these were absent, human experience would not be possible.

These three building blocks are principles, because there are no exceptions to them – they account for the entirety of human experience.

In other words, human experience is not a function of anything outside of us – not other people, not situations or events, not our past, not our future.

It is one hundred percent generated by these principles,

and is continually changing from moment to moment.

Syd knew that if people were to realize their experience – whether good, bad or indifferent - was only ever an effect of these three principles and nothing else, it could alleviate a lot of suffering.

It could save relationships.

Prevent wars.

It could unleash the creative potential of every human being.

My friend and mentor Jamie Smart inspired me to see an important distinction between thinking, thoughts and the principle of Thought:

Thinking and thoughts are what are created, the principle of Thought is what is doing the creating.

Thinking can look real. It can look important.

But it is only ever an output of the Principle of Thought.

Because Thought is endlessly creating fresh, new experiences, it means you are not limited to your current experience of life, whatever it might be.

You will naturally have new thoughts, and with those, new feelings and perspectives.

The more deeply we see that there is no intrinsic meaning in our thoughts, that they are nothing more than a momentary perception, we are free.

WHY THIS UNDERSTANDING IS DIFFERENT

Many self-help approaches and psychologies begin from the assumption that something needs fixing.
This understanding is different because its starting point is that we have nothing to fix.

Because we are derived from the same infinitely creative energy that everything in the universe is made from, we already have everything we will ever need to thrive in life.

The only thing that ever convinces us otherwise is our thinking.

The famed American author Mark Twain wrote,

"If we learned to walk and talk the way we learn to read and write, everyone would limp and stutter."

Just imagine for a moment teaching a baby to walk via PowerPoint.

Suppose for a second the baby can read and talk.

They might look at the slide deck and ask,

"Which foot should I start with, my left or right?"

"How far forward do I place it?"

"Which foot do I move next, the same one, or the other one?"

"How long should I wait before moving the other foot?"

"How high in the air should I raise it?"

"How do I balance?"

At some point prior to middle age this baby would be limping around and reading all the books they could about "Graceful Walking", the limp becoming ever more pronounced.

In our formative years, learning is very natural. We learn to walk by trying to stand, taking some tentative steps and then falling over. We do it again and again, until we have learned how to walk. No one tells us we must walk, we are naturally motivated to do it. And once we have learned to do it, we don't think about it. The ability to walk has become an embodied skill.

It's the same with talking. It's not something we feel we have to master, we just witness big people doing it and it seems like a good way of getting the stuff that you want. Our learning to talk is again very natural. We don't study how to make mouth shapes, or how to move our tongues, or how to coordinate the movements of our throat to project the noises we want to make.

We just open our mouths and make noises. We play with it. Some noises work. Others don't. We experiment, naturally.

Although we don't realize it at the time, these capacities are innate, in-built to the system, and our natural inclination for learning just brings them out when the time is right.

But somewhere along the way, we lose sight of this natural intelligence.

We get taught about the intellect and how to use it to direct thinking. We get taught there are things we should want, and how we can use our thinking to get these things.

We forget the natural intelligence that is always available and one hundred percent reliable - not only are you always learning, but the most intricate, complicated movements are being coordinated within you, every second of every day:

- If you don't think about your heart beating, does it stop?

- How many times have you missed your mouth with a fork recently?

- How do you balance when you walk?

When we buy into the idea that it is good to understand things intellectually, we begin to try and figure things out. We think about how we successfully achieved something -

a business goal, a great golf shot - and break it down into process steps, which, if followed precisely, will bring success every time.

But the world and our experience of it doesn't lend itself to this way of living, because everything is constantly changing. You and the world are subtly shifting in a billion different ways with every passing breath. No two moments are ever the same, even though it might feel like they are.

Our intellect is incredibly useful when used as a tool to give shape to the inner promptings brought to our attention by Consciousness.

But we also have a natural capacity to learn by being and doing, to absorb what we need to know, and put it into action.

Our intellect is responsive to what it knows. Our innate intelligence is responsive to the moment.

Whereas the intellect's expertise lies in evaluating the content of the known - our innate intelligence, our wisdom, is responsive to both the known and the unknown.

And this is how we continue to put one foot in front of the other, to breathe and to drive to and from work, even though our minds may be a tempest of worry.

You could say that innate intelligence and the intellect are like two people in a car, deciding on the best route. The intellect may contribute some interesting opinions, but our innate intelligence always remains the driver, and intellect the passenger.

WHY METAPHORS ARE SUCH POWERFUL CHANGE AGENTS

Metaphors are powerful change agents because they take as their basis everyday situations and images people can relate to.

They also highlight the number of parallels that can be drawn between humans and nature.

And that's the point. Human nature is so labelled because we are part of nature.

Forest fires renew the forests, just as our cells are continually regenerating.

Plants and animals have evolved to survive in the wild, just as human physiology has evolved over millennia.

As devastating as the after effects can be, volcanic eruptions are a release of intolerable pressure building within the earth's crust, just as we suffer physical symptoms when stress passes manageable levels.

The parallels between us and nature are everywhere.

Metaphors point to the connection that is ever present between us and everything around us, the connection that is there because we are derived from the same energy that everything around us is made from.

The infinitely creative energy, which means we live in a world of possibilities, if only we are open to them.

What enables us to embrace those possibilities, to be loving and optimistic, are the exact same things which cause us to doubt, be fearful and negative.

Our experience only ever works one way, being created moment to moment by three formless, eternal principles.

The principles of Mind, Consciousness and Thought.

The metaphors on the pages which follow are my attempt to draw parallels between our experience and our world, to highlight the unavoidable influence of these principles and the differences between how we believe life works and how it really works.

While Sydney Banks articulated three principles he also emphasised that really these were indivisible - three expressions of the same principle. Using three ways to describe the workings of the energy behind life simply makes this incredible power easier to understand.

Sometimes, I refer to all three. Mostly, I refer to just one, depending on what I think makes most sense, given the context.

Sometimes, I refer to Mind as innate intelligence, wisdom or infinitely creative energy.

Sometimes I refer to Consciousness as being aware.
The language is unimportant.

It will not be my words which will impact you, but the insights you may have while reading or reflecting.

Because you are made of infinitely creative energy, you are blessed with a limitless capacity for insight.

Take your time with these metaphors. Read a few at a time, and pause. Don't try to intellectually grasp them, just read and see what happens.

Some will resonate, some won't.

Those that do, may spark something inside which impacts your understanding of how life works.

These principles are the catalyst and the creator of your experience, and the more deeply you understand how your moment to moment experience is being created, the easier and more wonderful that experience becomes.

Enjoy.

THE METAPHORS

1

For anything to be a fact, it has to be true 100 percent of the time.

There can't be any exceptions. If there are, it's not a fact, but a measure of probability.

The ability of money, relationships, pain and anything else to determine our experience can be assessed by asking the question:

Does the idea dictate our experience 100 percent of the time?

For example, money cannot dictate our experience 100 percent of the time. If it did, poor people would always be miserable and rich people always happy – but they're not.

The same is true of all other ideas.

Sometimes a broken relationship can cause us pain. Sometimes it doesn't.

Sometimes a broken limb can prevent us from living life. Sometimes it doesn't.

In each case, the correlation between the idea and its ability to determine our reaction is less than 100 percent.

So it can't be a fact. That the correlation is less than 100 percent, means a person's experience must be being determined by something else.

What might this something else be?

Consider this question:

If Thought is not included, how is your experience coming to you?

You can name all manner of things - for example,

"My experience comes via feeling".

But how are you aware of that feeling, if not through Thought?

Try to find anything that can experienced without Thought - but do it without thinking.

If there is nothing which can be experienced without Thought, this means that experience is 100% Thought generated.

A principle.

A fact.

2

Mind, Consciousness and Thought work together to bring us experience in a similar way to how a DVD, DVD player and a television bring us a movie.

Mind is like the DVD player, containing the means of generating and projecting our lives.

Consciousness is the television, which brings this life to our attention.

Thought is the information on the DVD which is illuminated by the player and the television.

Like life, DVDs are designed to be enjoyed sequentially, providing a never-ending stream of images which pass before our eyes. As we watch we may feel happy, sad, we may laugh, or cry, but the images are not responsible for these feelings, because they have no inherent value – they are nothing but digitized projections from an inanimate disc.

The images are only brought to life by our use of the power of Thought.

At certain points while the DVD is playing, we may choose to press pause, re-play a scene or skip forward to one much further into the movie.

Whenever we do, we are interfering with the story's natural flow, and this is exactly what we do when we dwell on either a past experience or one which is yet to come.

We forget that we can only ever experience Thought in this moment, and kid ourselves that we are experiencing the past or the future.

But this is not possible. What we are feeling is not the past or the future, but a projection from within, and we are always experiencing it in the here and now.

When we realise our experience can never be determined by things outside, life is simplified and stress begins to subside.

We come to see thinking as inconstant, ever changing, something that doesn't need managing because it is designed to change, just as a DVD brings us forever changing images.

In the cinema of your mind there is an infinite archive of classic old movies (from various studios) waiting to be dusted off and played:

- The, "I Have A Big Nose So No-one Will Ever Love Me" movie
(Pixar World Apart)

- The "I Come From An Unhappy Home So Have No Choice But To Be miserable" movie
(Paramount Importance)

Then there are the movies about the future. These can be Utopian, Orwellian, or somewhere in between:

- The "If I Win The Lottery All My Troubles Will Be Over" movie
(Warner Bothers)

- The "I Have To Finish This Piece Of Work By Friday Or

The World Will Explode" movie
(21st Century FKUPS)

Whether the movies are happy or sad, funny or horrific, they all have one thing in common - they are as real as you believe them to be. You can be in fits of laughter at a comedy or scared stiff watching a horror film, but the moment you are reminded it's just a movie, the reality of it and the feelings provoked are popped like a balloon.

No matter how often we play these movies, whether they are a one-time special screening, or an extended run, they remain stories we made up.

But there is another option - to wander into an empty theatre which is showing something called:

"Watch this Space".

"Watch this Space" is a movie without trailers, because it has yet to be filmed. It is responsive to the moment, so all we have to do is sit back in our chair, jam another handful of popcorn in our mouths, and wait for the images to appear on the screen. The images play across our mind, and we simply think what we think and feel what we feel, because we have no preconceived ideas of what the film will be about or how we are supposed to react. We simply enjoy the experience and react in whatever ways occur to us in that moment.

And that movie is available to us, 24/7, 365, from the studios of Infinite Creative Potential.

4

The difference between the power of Thought and thinking is like the difference between the apple tree and its apples.

The apple tree is indifferent to whether the apples it produces are juicy and sweet, or hard and sour.

It does not judge itself as to the quality of its apples.

Its job is purely to keep on producing apples, just as the job of Thought is to keep on creating our experience of the world.

Thought has no judgement on what it creates.

Good, bad, indifferent - those are judgments we add by our own usage of this amazing power.

As we come to see the true nature of this creative power,

we can spend more time enjoying the wonders of the process and less time worrying about what is produced.

5

The Principle of Thought creates thoughts as the ocean creates waves.

We can no more change thoughts than we can waves. Trying to change thoughts would be like swatting at the waves with a baseball bat in an effort to disperse them.

The wave's nature is to ebb and flow, to oscillate and change form and the same is true of our thoughts.

Our task is to learn to surf our thoughts as we would waves, and as we do, some may seem more significant than others, some may cause us to lose our balance, or even fall from our surfboard.

But we always get back on and continue to ride and should never forget that in every moment, we are made buoyant by the ocean of wisdom that supports us.

6

The output of the principle of Thought is like the wind.

Sometimes it is a storm, battering and blowing you from pillar to post, other times it is a refreshing breeze, or a hint of movement in the air which barely brushes your cheek. Sometimes it is perfectly still.

It is infinite in its variability.

The energy from which the wind is formed is always there, ready to take form at any moment.

And thoughts are no different, for at source they are from the same formless energy as the wind.

Energy taking form in the moment and presenting itself as thoughts.

Where will the winds of thought take you today?

7

Thoughts are like fireworks, bursting into life across the skies of our mind in varying degrees of brilliance.

And then they fade away.

No matter how spectacular the firework may have been, there is no need to hold onto its memory, because new fireworks, bringing fresh illumination into your world, are right behind.

Thought is a never-ending firework display. There is nothing for us to do but enjoy the show.

8

Thoughts roll through Consciousness like stock prices on a television screen ticker tape.

The screen has no opinion of the information, it simply displays it. According to our investment in that stock, we are either delighted or dismayed by the value shown.

Just like thoughts, the value of the stock prices is arbitrary, made up numbers formed from the opinion of traders who are deciding, moment to moment, whether a company is worth investing in.

Those judgments are based on stories, opinions and what is "known" in the moment.

The stock price might slump on an unfounded rumour.

It might soar even as the CEO engages in fraudulent activity.

Until these stories come into the consciousness of the market, they have no effect on the stock price.

Take the Enron scandal of some years ago. The fiscal practices which brought the company down where just as prevalent while the company's stocks boomed. It was only when these practices became known that the company crashed.

Then there are our fears of the unknown, of what might happen in the future.

For example, Brexit. UK values and the pound slumped as the leave vote was confirmed. The value crash was based on fears of what might happen when the UK leaves the European Union.

But we can't know the future. If we did, we'd all be choosing the right lottery numbers every week.

Our experience fluctuates like stock as Thought creates the world anew. We then decide how to respond to this new world.

If we misunderstand where experience is coming from, we are likely to frantically interpret and react to every little change, but if we understand that experience is not reality but merely a projection of Thought in the moment - then no matter what the markets are doing, our stock will always remain high.

9

Thought includes everything that makes up our perceptual reality - what we can see, smell, hear, taste and feel.

Imagine you are on a train rushing through the countryside. Scenes of gently rolling green hills with cows contentedly grazing, give way to fields of sheep with new born lambs nuzzling into their mothers for comfort, then you are distracted by the aroma of a bacon sandwich teasing your nostrils, then the sound of a wailing baby startles you from your reverie.

Thought is continually refreshing our entire experience of life, every second of every day, and this is why we need never to feel defined or limited by anything.

It is why we don't have to fear our experience, or look anywhere else for an explanation of what we are feeling.

Thought ensures our perspective on life can and will change, naturally.

It's all part of the design.

10

Just as nearly 90% of an iceberg lies beneath the ocean's surface, so we as humans live from a submerged system of beliefs that have been built during our lives.

While it really does seem to us that these beliefs have come from influences like family, friends, society and media, look closer and you will realise your experience of these can only ever originate in Thought.

And as these blind spots are seen for what they really are, so they melt away, just as surely as an iceberg is melted by the sun.

11

You know how sometimes when you watch TV, you just know what you want to watch and other times you are aimlessly channel surfing?

Without us even noticing, the principle of Thought surfs through the channels of creation at all times of the day to bring us the information most relevant to the moment.

How aware we are of the information is influenced by how much thinking we are caught up in.

When we are clear minded, we are well attuned to the ideas, images and perspectives being brought to our attention. But when we are distracted it is not easy to focus on what's in front of us, just as it is not easy to settle on a TV programme when we are worrying about work or the kids.

What is the solution to cluttered or indecisive thinking?

To look in the direction of where it is coming from.

While it often looks otherwise, our experience is only ever brought to us by Consciousness and interpreted through the medium of Thought.

It only works one way, it always has and always will and once we understand this, we can take our hand off the remote, trusting in our wisdom to select whichever channel is most appropriate for us at that moment.

12

We are not our thoughts. We are the blank canvas on which our thoughts appear. We have a thought, and a picture develops. That picture will have more or less detail according to how much attention we pay to it.

When we get into difficulty, it is because we are mistaking that picture for reality. It is not reality, but a momentary representation of Thought.

For example, you might live in a mansion. Were you to buy a picture of a hovel, you wouldn't begin to believe that hovel was your true home.

Yet that is what we do with our thoughts every day. We forget we are the canvas, and think we are the picture.

If we believe it enough, we might try to change the picture, adding more and more layers to try and make the picture the way we want it. All this does is distort the image further.

When we believe what anyone else says about us, it's like buying their portrait of us and hanging it on a prominent wall where we can see it every day. But a portrait can never be you – it's just a perspective.

We don't have to work a portrait or appreciate it. We don't have to do anything with it, because a fresh, blank canvas is always available to us and our limitless potential for creation.

Thoughts have all the weight and permanence of air bubbles, dissipating as quickly as they are formed.

When we recognise that our thoughts are transient, we feel lighter.

Whenever life takes on a heavier feeling, you can be sure that it is because it looks as though your experience is being carved from something heavier than Thought.

It may seem that how you are feeling is being caused by a certain person, or circumstance.

But that is never case, because we can only know feelings, people and circumstances through thoughts - which form, float and pop momentarily - just like air bubbles.

14

I was once sharing this understanding with a mathematically inclined friend of mine, but it just wasn't happening.

The following analogy popped into my head:

"You know how when you multiply any number by a big number, the product is a big number, but if you multiply any number by zero, the product is zero?"

When he replied "Yes", I followed on:

"Well, thinking works the same way. You can have a few thoughts in your head, but if you give them a lot of value, you have a cluttered mind. You can also have a thousand thoughts passing through your head, but if you give them no value, you have a clear mind."

That helped him solve the equation!

15

Thoughts are like sandbags which act on the hot air balloon of clarity.

As we throw bags from the basket, so the balloon rises and we gain a wider perspective on the world.

Occasionally we may gather bags back in, causing the balloon to temporarily drift lower and narrow our perspective.

But we always have the option of throwing the bags from our basket.

We will never be sandbag free - as long as we are in the balloon we will always have them - but provided we don't take their presence to be a given on the balloon's ability to elevate, those sandbags will carry no more weight than they should.

16

Thoughts come to us like lottery balls on a Saturday night. They impact us according to whether or not they are one of our chosen ones. But even when the balls do not bring us joy, it's worth remembering there will be another draw very soon, another chance for a life-changing experience.

17

When the skies of your mind are darkened by storm clouds of thinking, it is easy to forget that the basic essence of the sky is cloudless. Thoughts are as permanent as storm clouds, and will soon pass.

Note: this does not apply to the storm clouds of Wimbledon fortnight.

18

Thought is like Frankenstein's Monster. It has no life of its own until animated by us.

19

Going through a particularly challenging day, I was reminded of the lovely analogy shared by wonderful Principles practitioner, Dr Bill Pettit:

"Thoughts are like unwanted relatives. If you do not feed them, they will soon leave."

20

As thoughts appear more or less relevant, so our perspective changes. The mountain we stand right in front of appears as a molehill when viewed from one hundred miles away.

Many years ago, we were holidaying in Chicago. It was a beautiful sunny day and my wife and I were enjoying strolling about the city seeing the sights and watching life go by.

It was hot and we realized how thirsty and hungry we were. We saw an intriguing looking restaurant and went in.

It was pitch black in there. I didn't think much of it and would rather have walked out, but my wife clearly didn't mind as she had gone on ahead.

In my rush to catch her, I walked right into a wall. My sunglasses fell off and I could see clearly.

I had completely forgotten that I was wearing glasses with lenses that adjusted to the light. We had gone from brilliant sunshine to a restaurant that was naturally lit, and the lenses had not had the chance to catch up.

Our feelings are never a commentary on the state of the world, they are only ever a commentary on the lens we happen to be looking through.

If we feel sad, it means we are looking through a sad lens.

If we are happy, it means we are looking through a happy lens.

The lens of Thought is continually adjusting, and as it does, so our experience changes.

We don't always remember we are wearing the lens of Thought, and that's why it is all too easy to believe that our experience is coming from the world beyond.

But remembrance of the lens is enough for our perception to begin to shift, and we are much less likely to walk into a wall!

22

People who are caught in an experience may believe things will never change.

But in doing so they are overlooking the fundamental nature of the human system - ever changing thoughts and experiences are part of our innate design, a natural ability.

Need proof?

Hold your breath for as long as you can.

Try as you might, sooner or later the system will override your efforts and force you to take another breath.

The system is designed to look after you - just as another breath is a given, so are new thoughts, and with them, new experiences.

23

Just as a needle on a compass shows which direction it is pointed in, so our feelings are measuring but one thing.

Just as a compass does not tell you about the weather, the time or your altitude, so feelings are not telling you about your circumstances, the people around you, your past or your future.

Your feelings are merely pointing to your true north, the actual source of your experience - your moment to moment Thought generated view of reality.

There is no separation between thought and feeling – they are two sides of the same coin.

Our experience of life only ever works one way - as we think, so we feel.

An elegant, simple, 100% reliable indicator, our own inner

compass, always seeking to reorient us towards our true north.

24

Often, we identify with our thinking and forget we are the embodiment of the principle of Thought, with fresh new ideas forming every moment.

It is like believing we are the vase, while forgetting we are the raw clay from which the vase is made.

25

Imagine you're a baker who loves bread, and you are very hungry.

Are you going to rummage in the bread bin among all the stale creations for something to satisfy, or will you turn to the oven to pull out something fresh?

When we go looking in our memory banks for an answer, we are rummaging around among stale creations.

We have a choice to turn to the known or the unknown.

The oven of the unknown - the formless principle of Thought - is forever ready with new creations perfect for the situation at hand.

26

Believing that the world can dictate how we feel is like a spider spinning a web and then forgetting it came from within her.

The web can be her best friend, helping the spider ensnare juicy insects, and it can feel like a trap from which she cannot escape.

But no matter how she feels about the web, it did not come from the outside world.

We use the infinitely creative power of Thought to spin our own webs.

When we forget they are of our own creation, we can easily suffer.

But once we remember, we turn towards the clarity and ease that is our birth-right and true nature.

27

Clarity of mind is less influenced by the number of thoughts in your head than it is by how substantial those thoughts appear to be.

When thinking looks important and a maelstrom of thoughts jostle for supremacy, it can feel like navigating your way through a room crammed full of sumo wrestlers.

Now fill the same room with five times the number of sumo wrestlers. To make your way through that room seems impossible.

Until you notice all the sumo wrestlers are holograms.

Now it seems very possible to cross that room.

When you believe you are experiencing the world and not the momentary projections of Thought, you can easily feel trapped.

But as you remember the true source of the projections, so their transparent nature is revealed and your breathing room returns!

Just as new characters in video games can be unlocked with skilful play, so insights unlock new ways of relating to life.

Before I learnt of the Principles, the character I believed I was lived in the feeling of circumstances.

As I understood more of the Principles, my new character came to see that I wasn't feeling my circumstances, but my thinking about my circumstances.

Since seeing the distinction between the Principle of Thought and thinking - the difference between what's creating and what's being created - it now occurs to me that I don't even necessarily feel my thinking about circumstances.

While my thinking might be related to what I happen to be doing, it might also be about something else completely!

Reflection is a great metaphor for the Principles, because the word speaks to the power of just allowing things to be, and seeing what comes through.

Dirty a mirror and the image reflected is less clear. Throw stones into a pond and what the surface reflects is disturbed.

But when the mirror or pond is untouched, the clarity of the reflection increases.

And so it is with Thought.

When we simply reflect, and allow ourselves to experience the natural stream of Thought, we find that what comes to us is context sensitive, designed for the moment.

30

Here's an example of how, as thinking changes, so does the world:

Vincent Van Gogh sold just one painting during his lifetime.

These days, if you want to replace the flying ducks over your mantelpiece with one of his masterpieces, it will set you back tens of millions of pounds.

While he was alive, Van Gogh was reviled, his work thought to be the product of a deranged imagination.

Now he is revered the world over, as one of the greatest artists who ever lived.

The paintings remain the same.

31

Trying to change our thoughts and feelings is like running after a bus which is disappearing into the distance.

Thoughts and the feelings are created before we are even aware of them.

But we need not fear when encountering thoughts or feelings we don't like, because these change without our doing anything.

Just as another bus will be along in a moment, so the Principle of Thought will bring us new thoughts and feelings.

The difference being, the timetable of Thought is 100 percent reliable!

32

There is no need to feel trapped by thoughts, because new thoughts happen just as surely as the ocean will wash away the name you've written in the sand.

Some believe the way to calm disturbing thoughts and feelings is to use a mental technique or a strategy – in effect, to calm the thought storm by adding another thought.

This is the equivalent of complaining of being too hot, and then putting on another sweater to get cool!

Trust in Thought to adapt to the situation as you trust in yourself to know when to add or discard layers.

34

Navigating your way through a confused mind is no different from driving through fog.

Know that fog is not the true nature of the sky, that in time it will naturally clear.

Until then, keep driving, use whatever light you do have and proceed with caution!

35

Quietening a turbulent mind can be like confronting a hurricane.

Fight a hurricane, and you will likely be tossed around in the whirling maelstrom, battered, bruised, and disoriented.

But relax, and allow the hurricane to take you where it will, and you may find yourself drifting into the eye of the storm.

As the storm continues to rage around you, here is a haven of peace and tranquillity.

So it is with us - engage with a thought storm, and you will be increasingly confused.

Don't resist, and you may find yourself dropping into a place of calm tranquillity.

36

Clinging on to a thought or a state of mind is like a beaver clinging onto a log for fear of drowning in the river.

The world of Thought in which we live is as much our natural habitat as the river is the beaver's.

The beaver doesn't need to cling onto the log – he just needs to remember that he can swim.

We tend to want to avoid the lows and hang onto the highs.

But if you are a musician and play only the high notes, how less varied and rich is your music?

Embrace both the high and the low notes – they are all a vital part of the beautiful symphony that is life.

Our self-correcting system is like the auto-tuner on a radio.

The tuner automatically scans for the frequency which offers the least interference and the best clarity of sound.

When we manually try to tune the radio, we often find it harder to find that frequency. The sound can be beset with distortion and interference.

The human system is no different. Too often, we interfere with a distorted signal and try to think our way to clarity, whereas, left alone, our auto-tuner will find the frequency most appropriate for the moment.

Our default mental state is one of clarity and ease. When we drop out of that place, it is all too easy to believe we need to implement a strategy to try and regain it.

That is completely unnecessary, for our mental well-being works in the same way as a thermostat regulates the temperature in a building.

The thermostat monitors the actual temperature in the vicinity and kicks in when it varies too much from the set temperature.

This is how our state of mind works. We have a mental thermostat which continually seeks to restore us to clarity.

Implementing a strategy to restore clarity is the same as feverishly adjusting the thermostat because the room temperature does not immediately change.

Just as the thermostat may take time to restore the ideal temperature, so our mental thermostat may take time to restore clarity to a mind which has been drowning in overwhelm and stress.

But restore it, it will, if left alone to work its magic.

40

Famous film directors like Steven Spielberg and George Lucas are much admired for their creativity.

Yet I can name many people who can make a movie from a single sentence.

They do so because of a simple misunderstanding of where experiences originate from.

We have a thought.

It means nothing.

We then create a whole story around that original thought, and give it life.

But when we realize the story only has the reality we create for it in our minds, we can do what we like with it – put it aside, film it, even create a trilogy from it – without believing it is a true commentary on the state of our world.

41

One day a boy picked up a book which told exciting tales of heroism.

The next day, he picked up a book which was delightfully funny.

The day after, a book that was tragically sad.

They were all the same book.

If an author writes a book which sells 20,000 copies, she has written at least 20,000 stories.

Because it is not so much what is written, as what is read.

Depending on our experience of Thought in the moment, a book can impact us in a myriad of ways. Some days it can look like a great book, some days not so much.

Because our thinking is so fluid and ever changing, as we journey through life and develop, we can even convince ourselves the book we are reading is a completely new version.

It's the same book, but as our thinking changes, so does the story.

42

One of my favourite books is *The Hitchhiker's Guide to the Galaxy* by Douglas Adams, because it is both hilarious and speaks very eloquently to the quandary of being human.

For those of you not familiar with the book, the story tells of the quest to learn the Ultimate Answer to Life, The Universe and Everything.

A race of pan-dimensional beings builds a super computer - Deep Thought - to calculate the answer.

After briefly cogitating for seven and a half million years, Deep Thought gives them this answer:

42.

The trouble being, Deep Thought says, that she was never exactly sure what the question was.

Find the question, she says, and you will understand the answer.

Deep Thought does not know this question, but builds a super computer which includes organic life within the operating matrix, to figure it out.

The super computer is known as The Earth.

The planet and all life on it is animated and so begins the quest to find the Ultimate Question to Life, The Universe and Everything.

I have yet to find a more convincing explanation of how we came to be here.

It speaks beautifully to our all too human dilemma – even when we do have the answer, if we don't understand the source, it won't make sense to us.

The characters are scared by the answer 42 because it doesn't make sense to them, just as we are frightened by our experience when we don't know where it comes from.

But as we deepen our understanding of where our experience comes from, so it becomes less frightening.

The characters never did learn the Ultimate Question to Life, the Universe and Everything, and sadly the author died before it could be revealed.

I have my own favourite theory of what that question

might have been:

"What do you get when you live life at sixes and sevens?"

43

Douglas Adams also theorized in *The Hitchhiker's Guide to the Galaxy* about the population of the universe. Not every planet is populated. The space which contains planets is infinite. Because any finite number divided by infinity is practically zero, this means the population of the Universe is also zero - so anyone you do happen to meet, is purely in your imagination!

Thought generates our experience of the entire universe, and the people within it.

There is nothing that can escape Thought, even when it seems so certain that it is coming from "out there".

"Out there" is still within Thought - otherwise, we couldn't experience it.

On the physical plane there are of course people, but on the spiritual plane we are the same, all springing from the same formless energy.

To that extent, the population of the universe can be said to be zero.

44

Just like movies, life is a stream of ever-changing images and sensations. Because of this, our understanding of the world is continually evolving. We are changing.

Sometimes it looks as though these changes are being caused by our circumstances, situations and relationships - but this is a trick of the mind, as such changes only ever result from a change in thoughts.

Often, we pretend that life is like a photo album, a series of moments frozen in time - we formulate images of who we are, of who other people are, of past events, as though these are static, never changing. It doesn't occur to us that these images are made from Thought in the first place, nor that our memories of the past are crafted from the perspective we have now – a perspective that might be completely different from the one we had at the time of the event.

We complain that our loved ones have changed. They complain that we have changed.

Of course we have changed, we can't get away from it - we are continually being updated by our moment to moment experience.

That is why although we may pretend that life is like a photo album, it will always be more like a movie.

45

Human beings seem to be like elastic bands, resistant to change and capable only of being stretched to a certain point before snapping back into shape.

But as our understanding of the human experience deepens, so the band is enlarged and will stretch further and further and further.

46

Suspend the most powerful weightlifter a few feet off the ground and he is able to lift next to nothing. Without grounding, he has no leverage.

As we increase our understanding of anything in life, the more grounded we become and the more we can impact the lives of others.

47

It's easy to think that we all see things the same way.

But the truth is thoughts are like snowflakes or fingerprints - unique, and this is why our experiences of shared situations can be so completely different.

48

There are those you will meet in life who will tell you they have no imagination.

To them you may ask the question,

"Have you ever had a nightmare, or feared something terrible would happen that never came to pass?"

I have yet to meet anyone who hasn't.

Folks who believe they have no imagination are missing the elusive obvious – their world is being created moment to moment by the power of Thought.

If you have that power – and everyone blessed with breathing does – you have all the imagination you will ever need.

You just imagine you don't!

49

We experience reality in the same way as light is refracted through a prism.

Light hits the prism and we perceive a myriad of colours coming out the other side.

With us, reality is refracted through the prism of Thought and becomes our experience.

As long as we do not confuse our experience with reality itself, we are free to enjoy whatever shows may dance across our consciousness, without feeling the need to take any of it too seriously.

50

Some time ago at work our boss handed us a photograph of a man sitting on a sofa looking at something.

We were asked to identify what he was doing.

The responses were varied and diverse – he's in a doctor's waiting room, he's having an argument with his wife, he's watching the TV......

But all that could be seen for sure, was a man sitting on a sofa looking at something.

Anything else, were just stories that folk had made up.

51

In dreams, the most unbelievable scenarios look real. Uncle Stan, a chartered accountant from the womb whose idea of a wild time is to hold the fork in his right hand, could turn into a beaver who tap dances the length of the Great Wall of China, and that seems totally cool.

It's only when you wake up, that you realize the dream for what it was.

Just a dream.

Not reality.

But some pretty ridiculous things also go through our heads during waking hours, which seem completely compelling and believable.

You spot a friend across a crowded street and because they don't return your wave, you obsess about what this says about your friendship.

Your gorgeous girlfriend has the temerity to look at another man in a bar and it's a sure sign she is inviting applications for your replacement. That the man is the bartender and she just wants a drink is neither here nor there.

Whereas we are unlikely to see our dreams as reality, we can be convinced that our waking thoughts are a factual commentary on the state of our lives.

In both cases, it is all too easy to overlook that what we are experiencing is a momentary reflection of Thought.

Whether or not we are asleep, we are constantly dreaming.

It's just a question of whether or not we are awake to that!

We are all fish in a river of wellbeing. Sometimes the current may push us closer to the surface, sometimes closer to the bottom.

But we are always immersed in and supported by the river. Sometimes, we forget this and thrash about, feeling as though we might drown.

But eventually the remembrance comes that you are in your natural habitat.

You are cared for.

Always.

Just like being human, if we were a lake, our daily life would have disturbances.

There would be ripples on the surface brought about by the weather, birds swimming, frogs leaping from lillypad to lillypad.

Sometimes we would freeze when it was cold.

Sometimes we might begin to evaporate when it was hot.

We might get besieged by algae.

Rocks might build up on our bed.

Being a lake, we would have no attitude towards these disturbances.

We would not feel these said anything about who we are,

or our true nature.

Disturbances would be temporary, as our true nature would be to be clear.

Like the lake, our true nature is to be clear.

Any disturbances which seem to contain important information about our nature are temporary.

Our disturbances are nothing but thoughts, only ever as permanent as the ripples on the surface of the lake, as fleeting as the path cut through the water by a gliding swan.

Being a drop of water in the ocean of life, humans are tidal.

Sometimes we are on the crest of a wave and other times we are in a trough.

We tend to want always to be on the crest, and to avoid the troughs.

In thinking this way, we are missing three things:

One - flowing from one part of the ocean to another is quite natural. There is nothing to be done to go from a trough to a crest, it will just happen.

Two - crests and troughs are merely surface fluctuations.

Three - beneath these surface fluctuations is a place of deep tranquillity which is ever present and always accessible.

Once set in motion, a spinning top finds its own balance point.

If we interfere, its smooth pattern of movement will be disrupted.

Humans are designed to auto-correct, and the less we interfere with that system, the more easily we will find our balance point, too.

Honouring the voice in your head which judges you, is like retaining a personal assistant who continually berates you.

While engrossed in our favourite soap opera, it's unlikely that we would shout at one of the characters for doing something bad, because we know it is all made up.

Our perceptions of the people we meet in everyday life are just as made up, and yet having an argument with them doesn't seem so mad.

Until we recognize the true source of our experience, we spend our lives chasing the hare.

Allow me to explain.

I've always heard that greyhounds are very intelligent creatures.

Creatures that spend a lot of time sprinting two laps of the track trying to catch the hare.

Which got me to thinking:

If a greyhound is so intelligent, what prevents him from realizing that, rather than chasing the hare, he can simply stop and wait for it to come back around?

He could saunter out of the traps, light a cigarette, read the paper and still have plenty of time to nab the hare as it comes by.

The greyhound doesn't have to catch the hare. The hare will come to the greyhound.

We're no different. Until we understand how the system works, we spend our time chasing the answers to our problems.

But we never have to.

If we allow them to, the answers will come to us.

59

Anytime you forget that circumstance does not dictate experience, take a look around a packed commuter train which is delayed.

There you will find the gamut of experience - the stressed businessman, another who is relaxed, lovers lost in each other's eyes, lovers lost in an argument, a wailing baby and a gurgling one.

It's the same train, and yet, so many different trains of thought.

60

When we choose to board a train of thought, it is as well to remember four things:

- You can board any train you like

- If you don't like where it is heading, you can get off

- You can always hang out on the platform for as long as you want

- There are an infinite number of trains you can board ready to take you to an infinite number of places*

*South West trains neither endorse the above nor believe it is any way representative of their service.

61

As human beings we tend to label things as possible or impossible.

But is anything truly impossible, or is it just that we don't have a deep enough understanding as yet?

In the 1930s, French Entomologist August Magnan used the principles of fixed wing aero dynamics to prove the bumble bee could not fly.

Fortunately, the bumble bee knew nothing about this and carried on flying regardless.

Magnan's assumption was the bumble bee flapped its wings up and down. But once science understood the bumble bee flapped its wings back and forth, it could see how the bumble bee could fly.

Whatever the subject, as we understand more, our

thinking changes, and consequently so does our view of the world.

We used to think the world flat, but now we know it to be round.

At least, it seems that way, according to our current levels of understanding!

62

Consciously trying to settle your thoughts is similar to forcing a cat into a box. Put a cat in a box and she will likely jump straight out. If you leave a box in a room where the cat can find it though, chances are she will settle down comfortably in it, all of her own accord.

63

Until we understand the true source of all experience we are, as Rowan Atkinson once said:

"Like the blind man searching the dark room for the black cat...which isn't there".

Labouring with the misunderstanding that we can feel something other than Thought, we spend our time desperately looking in the wrong places for whatever we seek. We might believe it's not where we are looking that's the issue, but how hard we're looking, or that we are not clever enough to figure it out.

There might be a million reasons, and no matter what disguise they happened to be wearing, all those reasons would be thoughts.

As we understand that we can only ever experience Thought, it's like we get laser eye surgery and can see again. We replace the light bulb in the dark room, so we can check that the cat is not in there and it intuitively occurs to us that the cat will be curled up in the box we tried to force her into yesterday.

We also notice she is ginger.

64

A famed aikido master was once asked how he never lost his balance when defeating a number of younger and stronger opponents.

He replied that he was frequently out of balance, but was always coming back to it.

He knew his balance was designed to self-correct, so didn't waste time fighting it.

He trusted in the natural design.

We want always to be in balance, but it is natural for that to ebb and flow.

The more we understand how the system works, the less we interfere, and the more often we will be in balance.

65

An aikido master will tell you never to resist an attack. The best response is to sidestep the assault and use the assailant's momentum to throw him away.

Resisting an attack enables the assailant to get a hold which creates tension. Resistance gives the attack power which destabilizes, robbing you of strength and balance.

Not standing in the way of natural momentum enables the assault to end quickly.

Our thinking works in a similar way.

When we engage in a thought we allow it to get a hold on us, and we can quickly become tense and destabilized.

Thinking might be obligatory, but engaging with thoughts is optional.

Sometimes we can't help ourselves – and that's a perfectly natural part of being human too.

Knowing that thoughts will naturally pass on by gives us our best chance of not prolonging the struggle!

66

My youngest daughter loves Minecraft. She will spend hours creating and exploring fantastical worlds full of castles, rollercoasters, fire pits, zombies and sheep whose sole purpose is to keep the grass short (the sheep, not the zombies).

At any moment she so chooses, she can change the world, exit from it, or even delete that version and begin another.

What's interesting to me, is that sometimes she gets really frustrated with one of her worlds because it's not going how she wants it to – she can't quite construct the rollercoaster in the way that she wants, or can't finish reading the paper for being killed by a zombie.

These worlds are completely made up, but can look important enough to cause her real angst.

We are all playing games in our heads all the time. It's just some look more like games than others.

But when we realize that the game we are playing is one being made up in our head, we can see that our experience is merely a function of how seriously we are taking that game.

We can then play all out, feeling the highs and the lows safe in the knowledge that we can step out of the game any time we want.

It always helps your performance to know what game you are playing.

Acting from the belief that your feelings are coming from circumstance, is like turning up to a cricket match with a hockey stick – it might work, but your chances of success are much greater with the right equipment.

When you know your feelings are only ever coming from Thought, you are well equipped to smash a few boundaries!

68

The game we are playing never defines us, for we are not the game, but the field on which it is played.

Thought is the ball, the players, the goals and the referee. It is Thought that determines how the game plays out and our reaction to it.

There are endless new games, endless new outcomes.

But whatever the outcome – win, lose or draw – the game does not define the essential nature of the field, which remains ready to stage whatever game is played next.

69

We are characters who make shadows on walls and then mistake those shadows for reality.

We then have a choice - to recognize them as shadows, or make them real, and spar with them.

Believing your troubles are coming from anywhere other than Thought is like yodelling in a mountain range and blaming the echo for the avalanche.

The noise doesn't come from over there – it comes from you.

Why do our experiences vary so much?

Because Mind is the ultimate kaleidoscope, refracting energy in billions of different ways, every moment.

Thoughts are like pinballs, which are released into the machine of our minds and ricochet around with abandon.

Sometimes they will score a high value, and sometimes a low.

Sometimes we will skilfully manage the maelstrom of a multi-ball, other times we will desperately struggle with just the one.

But whatever their impact and lifespan, sooner or later, all balls disappear between the flippers.

Another ball is released, and the game begins again.

There is always another ball.

Always another game.

The history of you is forever in flux.

As events move from the future, to the present, to the past, so our thoughts and feelings about those events change.

This is why a tragic occurrence can lose its sting over time and why the love of our life can become our biggest mistake!

But while it looks as though we really can experience the past and the future, look closely and you will notice we only ever experience one thing – the present moment.

The now.

Why do so many seek enlightenment, when within us all is the eternal flame of wisdom, lighting our path every moment of every day?

Because people misunderstand, believing that what they seek is without.

No-one is without.

What you seek is within, and always has been.

Realize that, and you will enjoy the true beauty of the flame.

Wisdom is the infinitely creative intelligence woven into every fibre of our being, the operating system that ensures our bodily functions continue working even when we are blissfully unaware of them.

It is the key to unlocking many of the doors we wish to pass through in life.

The key to Wisdom lies in realizing there is no lock and no door, so no key is necessary.

Wisdom is all around you.

You are wisdom.

Wisdom is the ultimate processor. The fastest computer doesn't come close. Within us, it is co-ordinating countless actions and impulses every second. Our hearts beat, we breathe, cells regenerate, we grow, we learn to walk and talk.

Yet despite the overwhelming evidence that there is an intelligence far greater than our personal one looking after our every need, it still seems to make sense to take charge of our thinking sometimes.

This is what Sydney Banks was pointing to when he exhorted us to "just listen".

To not try to commit to memory, interpret or figure out. There is no need. We are blessed with the ultimate processor, which is absorbing and interpreting everything so it can give us whatever we need, whenever we need it.

It is perfectly calibrated to life.

Learning to live from wisdom is like learning to drive a car.

At first everything is very jerky and conscious as you learn to use your mirror, signal, manoeuvre, position the car and change the gears. It seems you are running through a perpetual, cyclical check list, and if you were to stop for even a second, you would wrap the car around the nearest lamp-post.

But over time, each of these things becomes a little less conscious.

You'll be driving along and suddenly realize you are changing gears without thinking about it.

You realize you've not been conscious of your position in lane or hit a curb in ages.

You are getting an embodied understanding of how

driving works.

You are beginning to trust in your auto-pilot.

Learning to trust in wisdom is like this. At first, the idea that a subconscious intelligence is capable of co-ordinating our every need is a scary one.

And why wouldn't it be?

For years you have relied on conscious control.

You often overlook all the things that conscious control hindered.

You forget the millions of things your auto pilot takes care of – like sleeping and waking.

As you begin to learn about wisdom, you gain an ever-deeper appreciation for the design of the human system. Of how it's looking after you, without you even thinking about it.

Wisdom knows how to navigate you through life, and has been doing so every second of every day.

Wisdom is like a triangle in an orchestra. Not always easy to hear in a crescendo, but listen closely, and its sound can be heard, no matter how faint.

79

Wisdom is like a phoenix - no matter how badly we may be burned, at any moment our wisdom can lift us from the ashes of our past and take us in the direction of beautiful new experiences.

80

Wisdom comes in many shapes and forms.

It can come as a completely new thought.

It can be an old thought that you have recycled time and again.

But what differentiates wisdom is its relevance to the moment.

Like a bespoke suit, Wisdom is tailor made for the moment and just feels right.

The difference between living life from the intellect and living from wisdom is like the difference between a Chess beginner and a Grand Master.

The beginner struggles to understand what the next move might be.

The Grand Master intuitively not only understands the next move, but how the game may play out.

82

If you are around the same age as me, you may remember weebles.

Weebles were egg shaped toy people who would never fall down.
Our wisdom is like a weeble.

No matter what happens in our day to day lives, it is always trying to bring us back to balance.

Even in our darkest hours when it seems we are forsaken, it is working to restore us to health.

Whenever you are low, remember your inner weeble, and know that you while you may wobble, you will never really fall down!

There are two intertwined gears - a large one called wisdom and a smaller one called intellect - which work together to create our experience of life.

Most people misunderstand the relationship between these gears, endeavouring to have the smaller one drive the larger, not realizing the larger gear is already doing the driving, and always will.

84

The phrase "stream of consciousness" points to the capacity of our thoughts to flow like water through the river of our mind.

A river has no opinion about each drop of water, it merely allows them to flow freely as nature takes its course.

When we grasp onto a thought, we dam the river. The longer we hold on, the bigger the dam.

But the river continues to try to find the best course, no matter what debris and blockages it encounters along the way. If it can't remove obstacles, it will circumvent them.

We work in the same way.

Our wisdom endeavours ceaselessly to find the best course, no matter whether we aware of it or not, whether we are in the flow or consumed by obstacles.

It will always find a way, and is 100% reliable.

85

Joe had a work problem he couldn't solve. No matter how much he wracked his brains for an answer, one wouldn't come. Well-meaning work friends flooded him with suggestions, none of which helped. These just proved to be continual distractions which left him more and more confused.

He decided to go home, where it would be quiet. But his friends kept calling and sending emails. He refused to answer the doorbell, for fear it was another voice which would add to the cacophony.

At the end of the day he stepped away from the walls which were covered in process diagrams and flip charts, and flopped down into a comfy chair.

It had not been a good day. He had an urgent problem which needed an answer first thing in the morning and he was exhausted and no closer to a solution.

As he sat quietly reflecting, the doorbell sounded at the periphery of his hearing. Out of curiosity, he went and answered it.

There stood a kindly looking fellow, who looked vaguely familiar. The man simply said,

"Hello Joe, my name is Dominic, and I am a wizard. I know what your problem is and I know what the answer is. Would you like to hear it?"

When Joe nodded, the wizard explained.

Joe was at once flooded with feelings of relief and peace. The answer was simple, perfect and with hindsight, so obvious.

He and his visitor became great friends. Joe still has problems, but not as many as before and those he does have no longer seem quite as intractable. He knows he can always rely on the perspective of his constant companion, who Joe affectionately knows by the name of "Wiz Dom".

Scientists have written that if humans could travel at the speed of light, the whole universe would appear as one thing.

This would suggest that the faster we travel, the more we are able to perceive.

Spiritualists have written that intuitive perception is faster than the intellect.

Would combining these theories suggest that intuition is more perceptive than intellect because moving faster, it knows more of the universe?

We all spend inordinate amounts of time trying to fit the jigsaw pieces of our lives together.

The more I learn about how life works, the more I see my jigsaw is but a tiny part of a much larger one.

It's a bit like seeing what seems to be a picture of a piece of white felt, and then the camera zooms out and you realize you are looking at a herd of goats. Then it zooms out again and you realize that you are looking at a satellite camera's representation of a field somewhere in England.

We might be trying to fit the pieces of our life together, but our personal jigsaw is part of a puzzle with more than 7 billion pieces.

There is always a perfect place for us to slot in.

The best news is that we don't even have to try, because

we are part of a bigger Consciousness which is already piecing the whole puzzle together, moment by moment, and ensuring that we are right where we are meant to be.

By deepening our understanding of how life works, we will become ever more aware of the true picture of life and our place in it.

When we are quiet and reflective, it is much easier to get onto the same frequency as another person.

It is like being together in a room with the radio on.

When it is noisy, it is not always easy to hear the radio clearly.

But when quiet, when the radio is the only noise, we can both hear and enjoy it together.

89

The moment we try to capture an experience in words, we lose the essence.

Think of a stunning sunset which fills you with the most beautiful, indescribable feelings. You're sitting on a beach, a cool breeze caressing your cheek, while waves gently lap the shore. The backdrop to this is a sun casting a myriad of hues as it dips beneath the horizon.

Now try describing that sunset to another person.

You could use a thousand words but no matter how eloquent, they could never truly capture the experience.

Because the power is in the feeling, not the words.

90

Learning this understanding has felt like being in an empty room full of possibility.

Each insight has led me into a slightly bigger room.

I have another insight, and enter a bigger room, and so on.

The experience of insight seems to push the boundaries of what is possible further away.

Then one day it occurred to me that there are no rooms.

And no walls.

Just pure possibility.

The source of our unhappiness is misunderstanding.

The more we understand about life, the more we see the simplicity and effectiveness of its design and the easier it gets.

For example, many spend their lives trying to be extraordinary.

That is a wonderful aspiration, but the difficulty in achieving that state may lie in a misinterpretation of the word.

What if there is meant to be a silent space between the extra and the ordinary?

There is nothing to be added.

You are already perfect and have everything you need to

have an amazing life.

Be extra ordinary.

Human beings are like tuning forks.

When we speak from a deeply authentic place, the feeling we project resonates within the person we are speaking with.

They may not intellectually understand our words, but on some level, they recognize the truth of what we are communicating.

It is though we are ringing a DNA bell deep within them. Tell someone you love them in an angry voice, and will they hear love or anger?

Tell someone they are a silly fool from a loving place, and do they hear criticism, or love?

Allow yourself to become reflective, and listen for the feeling within.

It will tell you what you need to know.

It may not use words.

It's easy to lose sight of the connection between us.

The connection which is innate, because we are all the same energy, temporarily expressing itself in human form.

Interference in the form of thinking convinces us that we are separate beings, who are something other than expressions of the same energy.

In the spiritual realm oneness may be experienced, but not articulated, because once energy takes form it becomes physical, and the spiritual world can never be explained in physical terms.

It's like this:

We are all listening to the same webinar, but because of various interferences – dropped connections, persistent background noise and cross-talk because people are not muted and the like – it can seem as though we are on a conference call, where many separate individuals have a voice.

This causes us to lose sight of the fact that we are listening to a single person.

A single source.

We appear to be a body with a name and a history.

But experience of the physical world is created by our perceptions.

Perceptions are created by Thought.

Thoughts are as substantial as clouds.

As thoughts change, so does our perception of the world.

Our experiences, our bodies and all worldly forms are temporary.

The essence of all forms is the same energy.

And that is who we are –

The infinite, creative, formless energy that is the origin of everything.

If we are made of the same energy as all other forms in the universe, then any perceived separation is the illusion of form - because we think we are separate, we appear to be.

If separation is but the illusion of form, then the idea of a separate I is also a Thought created illusion.

That being the case, there is no separate I to enlighten.

In recognizing there is no separate I to enlighten, you are enlightened.

You always have been enlightened.

The only thing that convinces you otherwise, is your experience of Thought.

We live in houses, it's true.

But really we live in the SPACES between the walls, roof, floors, furniture and belongings.

The human body is a house, and we live in the spaces within.

Take away the house, and the spaces remain.

Reflect on this and you may get a glimpse of how fleeting form is.

No form is eternal.

There was a time when all the buildings in your town were not there.

A time when there was no town there – no buildings, and no people.

It was all space.

And what is this space?

The energy which makes up the universe.

The energy which gives form to the buildings and the people.

Though the form may pass, the energy remains.

The energy which is you.

The energy which is without beginning and without end.

Which means the energy that is you has always been there, and always will be.

In a sense, you were never born, and will never die.

Still worried about that electricity bill?

97

Many are the things taught to us in childhood which at the time appear innocuous but in fact point to the secret of life.

A little song which many a mum has sung to their child popped into my head the other day:

"Row, row, row your boat,

Gently down the stream,

Merrily, merrily, merrily, merrily,

Life is but a dream."

At birth we are given the vessel of our body, which is launched into the stream of life.

On the journey, we need never expend any more energy than is necessary. We can be gentle, because the stream will take us to where we need be, when we need to be there. Along the way we will be continually greeted by new sights and experiences, because we are only ever in the same place momentarily.

Sometimes the journey will seem very serious, because we don't like what we see and it looks so real.

But in truth we can be light hearted about it, because our experience is always ever, only, a dream.

Here is an old Buddhist story that beautifully illustrates the truth of our innate well-being:

A young man owned a clay statue, a family heirloom. He had long wished that it were gold, instead of dull, brown clay. When he began working, he saved his money so he could have the statue covered in gold.

He was proud of the statue, and enjoyed the admiration it inspired in others when they saw it. But it was not long before the gold plating began to flake off. The young man had it plated again, and again the gold flaked away. Soon all his time and money was being spent maintaining the gold facade.

One day his grandfather returned from a long journey. The young man wanted to show him how he had turned the clay statue into one of gold, but was embarrassed by how the clay showed through the gold.

The old man held the statue with great care and gently rubbed it with a damp cloth. As he did, the clay began to dissolve. He said to his grandson,

"Many years ago, the statue must have been dropped in the mud and been covered in it. Not having seen it before, you just took it to be a clay statue. But look!"

Where the clay had been, a bright golden colour shone through.
"The statue has always been solid gold. It never needed more gold to be put on. Remove the clay and you reveal the gold statue that has been yours all the time."

If we misunderstand our true nature, it might make sense to gold plate what we have, leading us on a wistful, time consuming and often expensive journey looking for fool proof ways of doing this.

But no matter how good the strategies we apply and the facades we create, the effect is at best temporary. Sooner or later the strategies and facades will flake, because this is nature's way of hinting that we do not need to fix something which is not broken.

Instead, we merely need to recognize that we already are that which we are looking for and as we understand this, the mud of thought will fall away and the brilliance of our innate well-being will again shine through.

I'm a big fan of the cult sci-fi TV series Dr Who.

Many years ago, there was a story which featured Omega, a being so powerful it took three incarnations of the Doctor to combat him.

Omega wore a fearsome mask, and in obliging the Doctors to kneel before him, he exhorted them to look upon the true face of Omega.

But when Omega removed the mask, there was nothing behind it.

Omega the being was nought but a collection of beliefs which he convinced himself had reality in the world of form.

In a physical sense, he was absolutely nothing.

Or to look at it another way, he was absolutely everything, composed of the same formless, infinitely creative energy which is the source of all things.

We all wear different masks on different occasions.

But what lies beneath the mask?

100

The late comedian Michael Bentine once received a letter from a seven year old boy that he had framed and hung on his office wall:

"Dear Mr Bentine, I love your television programmes, but I prefer your radio ones because the scenery is better."

This beautifully speaks to the state of mind that seems so natural to children and their unending ability to create amazing worlds.

Very young children tend to follow their inclinations. They pay attention to what their elders say – sometimes – but are far more interested in doing what makes sense to them in the moment.

For them, life is a laboratory of fun. Some things turn out great. Others blow up in their face.

They laugh and they cry. They have emotions, but emotions do not have them for long. They move on and tend not to be defined by their experiences.

As we get older, it seems we lose this ability. We think we have to take things seriously. We have exams to study for and pass, commitments to honour, jobs to go to and eventually, families to look after.

Our laboratories are more serious. We experiment less, and the experiments we do are more controlled and we are prone to be defined by their conclusions.

We are educated that life works in a certain way, that certain things are right and certain things are wrong. Conform with the majority view, and you are ok. Intelligent. Sensible.

Go against the grain, and you are strange. Weird. An outcast.

Although the worldview we adopt may come from our families, society or our jobs, our experience of it comes from the exact same source that created the wonderfully imaginative worlds of childhood.

It comes from Thought.

The world created in your head at the age of 45 is no less imaginary than the world created in your head at the age of 5.

There is nothing innate about getting more serious and tense as you grow older.

That is merely a made-up idea you bought into.

It's a thought.

You still have access to the imagination, creativity and sense of fun and laughter you had when you were small.

We are all kids. We are just a bit bigger now.

Now there's a thought!

101

Another reflection on the letter Michael Bentine received from a seven year old boy preferring his radio shows to his television programmes because the "scenery is better".

A TV show or a movie gives you the director's view of the story. The version of the story being created in your head is influenced by those visuals.

A book takes away the visual element, so a novel of that same TV show or movie may be a completely different experience.

For example, I loved the movie *One Flew Over the Cuckoo's Nest*, but it wasn't a patch on the novel.

There are dream sequences in the novel that film is yet to do justice to.

I had no prescribed visuals, so those had to come from my

imagination.

To me, this speaks to what teachers are pointing to when they suggest to not listen to their words, but to your own innate wisdom.

Because the scenery is better, and more appropriate for your needs in the moment.

102

Because we humans all think differently from one another, we live in separate realities.

Not realizing this is a huge source of misunderstanding. We tend to assume that everyone sees it as we do, but the truth is, there will always be differences, no matter how small.

One of the best ways to build relationships and create great feelings is to develop a better understanding of how someone else sees reality, and to remember that their reality is changing with their thinking, too.

Differences can cause misunderstandings, but are also the source of much joy.

Take humour – so much of it is based on misunderstanding.

For example, I give you a joke from one of my favourite films, *The Pink Panther Strikes Again*, which features the incomparable Peter Sellers as the bumbling detective, Inspector Clouseau.

Clouseau walks into a hotel and asks for a room.

As he does, he notices a cute dog by the reception desk.

He asks the receptionist,

"Does your dog bite?"

The receptionist shakes his head and says,
"No."

Clouseau pets the dog, which sinks his teeth into Clouseau's hand and mangles it.

Shocked and hurt, Clouseau turns to the receptionist and says,

"I thought you said your dog does not bite?"

To which the receptionist responds,

"That...is not my dog."

It's a classic case of separate realities. Because the dog is sitting near the receptionist, Clouseau assumes the dog must belong to him.

It's a great and painfully funny example of how Thought creates our world, how often we mistake that for reality, and how quickly our reality changes as we get a deeper understanding!

103

"The greatest trick the devil ever pulled was convincing the world he didn't exist."

This memorable line is uttered in the movie *The Usual Suspects* by Roger Kint, a suspect being questioned by the LAPD about a heist gone wrong which led to the murder of a crime gang member.

During his interrogation, Kint weaves a compelling story of a shadowy, malevolent figure behind the heist - Keyser Söze, of whom all the other gang members were deathly afraid.

According to Kint, none in the gang knew who Söze really was - but that he was definitely the murderer.

Kint seems an unlikely criminal, a hunched over, nervy character debilitated by cerebral palsy.

After extensive interrogation, he is released by the LAPD. Kint begins limping back to his car, but the further he gets from the police department, the straighter his gait and the faster and longer his stride becomes.

It turns out he was Keyser Söze all along. He did an amazing job convincing people otherwise.

Thought does an amazing job in convincing us that our experience is coming from somewhere else, that it is not the guilty party.

It disguises itself so cleverly that we can be fooled for years into believing that all manner of elements outside of us are most likely to be responsible for our feelings.

This innocent misunderstanding causes us to believe we are separate from the experience, the victim of it.

But the truth is without the capacity to be aware and to think, we can know nothing of these external factors. We can have no experience of them. Experience is always an inside job.

Look past the usual suspects and look to the one that so often looks the least likely.

The greatest trick, indeed.

104

There's a wonderful moment in the movie *Witches of Eastwick* when one of the "witches" complains about the unfairness of life, to which Jack Nicholson's Devil character responds:

"Well, we don't deal the deck down here. We just play the percentages."

Thought is continually dealing us a fresh hand, moment to moment.

We get in trouble when we try playing a hand from our past, or one we anticipate getting in the future.

The percentages on those hands are terribly low, because they have no relevance to the moment.

Yet we spend so much time and energy trying to play those hands.

When we live our present hands, we become alive to the possibilities in them.

The percentages rise.

The more we recognise how the game really works, the better our chances of turning our present hand into a winning one.

You're contemplating a tightrope stretched across the Grand Canyon.

The sweat pours as you think about your certain death if you make one false move.

The mist shrouds the canyon below you; you cannot see where you will fall.

The uncertainty only makes you feel worse.

As you stand frozen to the spot, the mist begins to clear and you notice the safety net below.

You might fall a ways, but the net will catch you before the ground does. You'll survive.

You relax a bit and move to edge your way across. As you do, you become aware of the safety harness tethering you to the tightrope.

If you fall, you won't fall far. You can recover. It won't be easy, but it's possible.

As you stand there considering your next move, you notice you are still on solid ground.

Psychologically we are always on solid ground, it's just that sometimes, we think differently.

Deepening your understanding of how life works is like trekking up a mountain.

The path will not always be smooth.

Sometimes the way we must take will be obvious, and other times it will be difficult to know.

Sometimes because of the rocky terrain, the path may take us lower again, before we can continue on upward.

Sometimes the vistas will take our breath away.

Sometimes the vistas will be hidden by the mountain, or the surrounding foliage.

Sometimes we will be energised and bound along.

Sometimes we will be worn out and need to rest.

But we always remain on the path.

Once we reach the summit, we will enjoy an unobscured panorama.

Occasionally these beautiful views may be lost to us, as we are enveloped in clouds.

We can always take solace that while we might not be able to see clearly, we may be right where we want to be - and that at any moment, the clouds will lift and we will once more be able to see for miles and miles.

There was a famed author who throughout his career had written many a best-selling and much-admired book.

Yet there was one work of his which divided opinion. Some loved it, and heaped praise on him for his ingenuity and intelligence. Others hated it, and poured scorn on it, even going so far as to question whether his writing skills were as good as they used to be.

He continually revised this work, in the hope of winning universal approval. But the more he worked on it, the more opinion divided.

He became more and more frustrated and conflicted by the whirlwind of opinion which seemed to bind him.

Then, one day, he woke up and knew what to do.

He would let the book be.

Let the opinions be, for they were simply opinions and not truths.

As for the characters who had voiced the opinions, he didn't have to be unduly swayed by them.

He had, after all, written them himself.

108

Jack was lost. Diving into the maze had seemed such a good idea, because he had a problem and for all the world he was sure the answer lay in there.

But the deeper he delved into the maze, the more confused and uncertain he became. He had forgotten how he entered, and could no longer retrace his steps.

He still felt that what he needed lay somewhere within, so it made sense to him to plough on, deeper and deeper.

But the longer this went on, the more desperate he became.

He started to run faster and faster, but this only increased his confusion and made him feel tired. When he had entered the maze he had a sense of direction and purpose, but these had faded as time went on.

Jack stopped for a moment to catch his breath, and had an idea. Maybe he could rip his way through the maze. But he only had his hands, and the hedgerow walls were thick and thorny and quickly cut him.

Then he thought to climb the maze walls, to get a better perspective, to see his way out. In doing this he glimpsed the exit, but he grew tired of clinging to the hedgerows and fell back to the floor.

He lay there feeling exhausted - so much so that, without even deciding to, he began resting.

As he did so, a strange thing happened. The maze walls began to change shape. They began to shimmer and fade.

Jack found himself sitting on his living room couch, surrounded by his family, a warm mug of tea to hand and his faithful dog looking at up expectantly at him.

The maze was - and only ever is - made of Thought.

109

Two men are in an elevator. The button for floor 100 - the CEO's suite - is already illuminated.

One of the men is Mr. Corporate. He wears a sharp suit and accessories, is immaculately groomed, with an imposing yet fashionable briefcase. His face is a portrait of stress.

Under his breath he mutters, "Gotta get to the top, gotta get to the top" and as he does so, is persistently punching the button for the top floor.

But the more he presses that button, the more buttons for the lower floors are illuminated.

His efforts are causing the progress of the elevator to be slowed.

Exasperated, he turns to the other man, who is avuncular

and kindly in appearance, with a neat, bushy beard. This man very gently stays Mr Corporate's hand and says in a soft Scottish burr,

"Why don't you just enjoy the ride?"

This gentleman then quietly explains that the elevator works on the Divine Elevation principle, and that, left alone, the elevator will naturally go wherever you need to go, but if interfered with, will likely stop on floors you would rather not be.

As he journeys with the wise gentleman, Mr. Corporate comes to see that while they been sharing the same elevator, their experience of it is very different.

He sees a critical distinction.

He had always wanted to get to the top, but now he understands what is doing the elevating.

110

Coming to learn about the gifts that are naturally yours is a bit like being shown around a grand house by a wrinkled retainer.

To begin with the house is dark and as you wander around it, you have no idea what is within.

You simply know that you have inherited it.

The caretaker has a torch, and as he shines the torch around, you begin to get glimpses of untold valuables.

As you become increasingly accustomed to the light, you see more and more clearly that these valuables are everywhere.

What's more, they are all yours.

They always have been, and always will be, whether you

can see them, or not.

Imagine being an actor and getting so involved in the role you are playing, that you become convinced you are the character.

Although the character is made up, you would feel the same highs and lows, joys and sadness, as if you were that character.

This is exactly what we do when we buy into the idea that our thoughts depict the true state of ourselves and our world.

We are no more the character of our thoughts, than an actor is the character reflected in the make-up mirror.

There are an infinite number of roles we can play, and we are never limited to the one we might inhabit in the moment.

We spend our lives searching - for relationships, for love, for meaning and for ourselves.

What if, rather than searching for things, we are innocently hiding from them?

What if, in this cosmic game of hide and seek, we already have that which we are looking for?

What if we are made of love, with a limitless capacity to have a relationship with anyone and on some level already know the meaning of life?

What if we already are everything we will ever need for a wonderful life?

What if the only thing that ever separates us from the truth of who we really are is an intricately woven cloak made of Thought?

113

There is nothing factual about concepts such as good and bad, high and low - these are really personal judgments about a situation.

Here are a couple of examples:

You and I support opposing football teams. Yours wins, mine loses. You are happy, I am sad.

You could ask the question, "At what temperature does it get cold?" Ten degrees centigrade might be a heat wave to an Eskimo, but freezing to an Aboriginal.

In both scenarios, the situation is the same for those involved. What makes the difference is the thinking that each individual experiences in that moment. Even if a situation remains the same, new thinking can make it into an entirely different experience. For example, my football team losing these days is far less painful to me than it used to be, because it just doesn't seem as important to me as it once was.

Which, being an Aston Villa and England fan, is probably just as well!

114

People who struggle sometimes say they cannot find the meaning in life.

Or that life has no meaning.

It is one of life's ironies that when they are in such a state of mind, the person does not realise how close they are to truth.

Since we relate to life through Thought, life only has the meaning we give it and because of that, we all see it differently.

The meaning life has for us can change at any moment.

We can't avoid it. Our view of the world changes imperceptibly from moment to moment, even if we are not aware of it.

We are only ever one thought from the truth, and often that truth can be hidden in plain sight in the thoughts which, in the moment, cause us such pain.

115

A man went to the Ganges river, famed for its mystical healing powers.

When asked by a local sage why he had travelled so far, the man replied,

"I come to bathe in the Ganges so that I might be cleansed of all my sin."

The sage nodded – sagely – and observed:

"A donkey may bathe in those waters, but he will not emerge from them a horse."

In similar vein, many try to cleanse themselves of thinking, but this is futile – as long as we are human, our experiences will be crafted from Thought and we are powerless to prevent that.

We will have good moments and bad, happy moments and sad.

But the more we recognise that the daily ebb and flow of thoughts and feelings are perfectly natural - the more comfortably we will be able to bathe in the waters of life, without feeling compelled to be transformed in any way.

The problem with self-improvement models is they are based on a fundamental misunderstanding - that there is a self to improve.

For what is a self, except for a collection of thoughts you have about yourself?

I'm not suggesting that you do not exist, or that there is no world out there.

Last time I tried living on that basis, I tripped over a table and went ass over tip.

As we see how our experience is always changing from moment to moment, we see the temporary nature of thinking.

We begin to see how our idea of self is mind-made, a concept that is being continually updated as we live life.

One day we might do something wonderful, and feel awesome.

The next we do something we think of as stupid, and feel terrible.

Our image can also live and die by what others think of us.

But whatever may be feeding our concept of self, it is never coming from anywhere other than Thought.

In other words, our self-image is a Thought generated illusion.

The more we see that, the less time we will spend on improving the "self".

Sure, there will be times when we forget it's an illusion, and it will seem as solid as the table we tripped over.

But once you have seen through the illusion, you can never forget it.

It's like walking into a hall of mirrors at the funfair - you may not always like your reflection, but given where it's coming from, does it really make sense to spend time trying to change it?

I was listening to an excellent podcast recently on the topic of "Work-Life Balance".

When the host Michael Neill asked guest Robert Holden why he preferred referring to this as "Life-Work Balance", Holden's response went something like this:

"Because life is more important".

Work-Life balance.

What at first seems an arbitrary ordering of words looks more significant as I sit with it, a comment on the subtle and insidious influence that language and culture have.

Work first, life second.

Think about that for a moment.

Is there life after work?

Yes, for sure.

Is there work after life?

Not that I'm aware of.

Calling it a Work-Life balance implies there is a separation between the two, a separation which doesn't exist.

Dusting off the Venn diagrams of my youth, work is not separate from life, it's not even an intersection.

It's a subset of life.

Is there a principle which tells us that work is separate from life?

That it is less enjoyable?

I don't believe so.

We make up conventions all the time - and this one implies that work is unenjoyable, while life is a never-ending conveyor belt of beer and skittles.

To anyone with a modicum of life experience, this is clearly not true.

We have great days in life, and not so great days.

We have great days in work, and not so great days.

As human beings, we relate to our world through our ability to think.

As Shakespeare wrote,

"There is nothing either good or bad, but thinking makes it so."

Situations are not intrinsically good or bad, just as work is not really separate from life.

The separations we perceive and our categorization of things are simply our attempts to intellectually understand life.

We will always have preferences, but the more we realize our experiences cannot be separated from Thought, the more we can have these experiences without needing to categorise them, to separate them out from life.

Anytime you lose sight of how the human experience works, go easy on yourself.

Anytime you feel low, angry, or upset, give yourself a break.

As my friend Garret Kramer says, the human experience is a rollercoaster.

Even when we know how it works, we still lose sight of it from time to time.

Sometimes your head is clear, and sometimes your thoughts swirl like a ferret in a washing machine.

Sometimes you're up, and sometimes you're down.

Sometimes we feel happy, sometimes we feel sad.

Sometimes it will look for all the world that some person, circumstance, or event – past, present or future - has dominion over how we feel.

Sometimes we will be absolutely convinced we are right and others are wrong, mistaking our opinion for fact.

Sometimes we will forget that others see it differently, for they too are walking around in their own Thought generated reality.

We can be absolutely convinced we are feeling something other than Thought.

So what?

It happens to us all, and will do every day of our lives, because we are human.

All it takes is to be reminded of where experience really comes from, our mind will clear and we will be better equipped to deal with the ups and downs, which are, after all, part of the rollercoaster of life.

As I was beginning to learn about these principles a few years back, I mentioned to my friend and mentor Dr Aaron Turner that my head seemed noisier than ever. Rather than progressing, I felt I was backsliding.

He smiled and told me "That's good."

After my jaw incurred a few friction burns from bouncing up and down off the carpet, he continued:

"It's good because it means you are becoming increasingly sensitive to the noise in your head. Before, that noise was normal, so you never really heard it. But your thinking is getting quieter, so noisy thoughts are now sounding louder."

As I've continued my journey, I've seen the truth of this. Periods of beautiful peace are shattered by noisy, chaotic goings on in my cranium. These are often thoughts that never seemed important before.

Then I realize:

"Oh, I'm getting quieter again."

As you go deeper into this understanding, you will find yourself experiencing ever greater periods of peace and quiet.

It's a bit like living in the city and then moving to the country. In the cacophony of city life, it can be hard to hear the birdsong, but when you move to the country, it seems to be all around you.

As you continue your journey, when it does become noisy up there, be open to the possibility it's not a sign that you're backsliding, but of the increasing peace of mind that is becoming your new normal.

120

Our family lived in America for a time, and when travelling around we used to see amusing phrases on billboards outside churches.

One of my favourites was:

"When life makes you crazy, don't worry, even Moses was a basket case."

Because Thought brings ever changing experience, we can go effortlessly from one emotion to another - from happiness to sadness, love to anger, intensity to indifference.

Sometimes we seem to fluctuate from one end of the emotional spectrum to the other on a moment to moment basis.

It can indeed feel as though we are a basket case.

But because of the way our experience is truly created, this is perfectly normal.

One time, Syd Banks was talking about this and said,

"Everyone is schizophrenic...it's just some get a little bit more than others and get labelled schizophrenic."

This is not to deny mental suffering, but to point out that anyone is capable of any kind of thinking.

You are not so different from the most enlightened people as you may think.

Enlightened folk are subject to the same volatility of thought that we all are. They are just more comfortable with it, and spend less time dwelling on it. They understand where this volatility comes from, that it has no inherent meaning.

They know that maintaining mental equilibrium is nothing more than an understanding of how experience is created.

They know that we really are all the same. It is only ephemeral nature of thinking that convinces us otherwise.

121

My wife and I were on holiday in Italy, wandering along the path which leads to the rim of Versuvius, when I was struck by how lush and verdant the forests are which cover the mountain and the surrounding area.

Versuvius is infamous as the volcano which obliterated the city of Pompeii and its inhabitants in AD79, burying both in volcanic ash for 1600 years.

It has erupted with varying violence many times over the centuries. The poisonous gases which spew forth destroy the surrounding vegetation, just as surely as they destroyed Pompeii.

Yet nature rebounds. The trees regrow, and again cover the mountain sides.

We humans are blessed with similar resilience. No matter what happens to us, our nature always seeks to rebound and restore our default, which is one of growth.

We don't have to try to rebound from misfortune. Rebounding is inbuilt.

While volcanos can devastate, they are not inherently evil, being earth acne, weak spots on the earth's crust where pressure builds. When the pressure can no longer be contained, there is an eruption.

Scientists continually monitor for signs of an imminent eruption - an increase in smoke emissions, rising temperatures, bulging within the crater.

We humans are blessed with an early warning system - our feelings, which are a one hundred percent reliable guide to the thoughts running through our mind. If we are experiencing cool, calm feelings, we are having cool, calm thoughts. Explosive feelings mean explosive thoughts.

If we do explode, it is not a commentary on our nature. It just means we misunderstand what our feelings are telling us. We might think they are informing us about the situation and so we act accordingly, with consequences.

When we see how changeable and insubstantial thoughts are, we realize we don't have to act on them. We can allow them to pass, and see what comes next.

I'll admit to being disappointed when I peered into the crater of Versuvius. I was hoping for some bubbling magma, or at least an evil looking hole.

Instead, all I saw was a few trees, on a very ordinary looking valley bed.

The volcano has healed.

One day it will erupt and again bring devastation to the surrounding area.

And in time, the volcano and the surrounding area will heal again.

Just as we can live safely in the knowledge that no matter what we may be feeling, no matter what we may be thinking, whatever happens, we will heal.

It's our nature.

122

My eldest daughter lives life to the full, and that includes the daily dramas of her pre-teen existence - not being able to go shopping for the bag she must have right now, what so and so said about her in an Instagram yesterday and what it says about her popularity among her peers. She can also be incredibly kind, playful, loving and grateful.

She often vacillates between exultant joy and abject misery on a seemingly moment to moment basis.

In this of course she is no different to any other person who breathes - as her thinking changes, so does her experience of the world, even though there may be no difference in the outward circumstances.

My daughter will get a discomforting thought and seeing it as a commentary on her situation, leaps on the thought train and goes wherever it takes her.

The time she spends on the particular journey and how

perilous it seems to her varies.

Occasionally I might suggest to my daughter that she's not seeing things as they really are.

This usually results in the train speeding up.

Just as it's not a good idea to try to persuade a passenger to jump from a speeding train, so it doesn't work to try to persuade someone to jump from a runaway thought train. Both are moving too fast. The only way someone can safely disembark from a train, is for it to first slow down.

How is the thought train slowed down?

By not doing anything to speed it up.

The train will come to rest.

It might not be straight away. It might take a while.

But it doesn't work to try and persuade my daughter that her view of the world is wrong.

She thinks what she thinks and feels what she feels, and the view out of the train window looks real enough to her.

When MY thought train is moving at a speed I can see things clearly, I might offer her a cuddle, an ear, to just be with her, or leave her be.

From this place, I do whatever occurs to me in the

moment, as I know that wisdom has the infinite capacity to give me exactly what I need for the situation at hand.

In time, without being continually re-stoked, my daughter's thought train does slow down.

Once I can see she has disembarked, we can talk.

I can point to where her experience is coming from.

While it might look like her perspective is being shaped by the world outside her window, it is always a momentary creation of Thought.

I can't say for sure whether what I'm saying is having an impact.

But I do know that she hears me.

Soon she will board another train, which will take her to destinations and experiences unknown.

But the destination is not the important thing.

The important thing is she knows where her experience originates from. As long as she does, her innate wisdom will guide her to whichever train serves her needs best in the moment.

Then she can take the journey, without the journey taking her.

123

Every now and again we have decisions that look very difficult.

But how difficult are they really?

When you think about it, we are making decisions every second - when to get up, whether to make a cup of tea, to rush to catch the next train or saunter to the one after, which direction to take, even where to put our attention in the moment.

Some days, decisions look easy. Some days, they look hard. Some days the decision that looked hard yesterday, looks easy today. Decisions that look tough to us, look simple to others.

As thinking ebbs and flows, so the difficulty of the decision changes.

Once I was recruiting a member for our work team with two colleagues.

We had two candidates whom we loved, but we couldn't choose between them.

We were agonizing about it.

At some point my deeper intelligence peeked through the dense fog of my thinking -

"If we love them both so much, we can't go wrong. Either is a great decision".

We pretend we know how things will play out.

But we don't. We can't.

We make the best decision we can in the moment and then see what happens.

Frequently we act as though a decision is final, that we can't go in a different direction afterwards. We get it in our heads that to change our minds shows indecision and weakness.

But if we have new information which suggests a better direction than our previously chosen one, doesn't it seem sensible to act on that?

I'm reminded of an interview I read with a NASA engineer, who was being asked how difficult it was to calculate the correct path for a lunar module to land safely on the moon. He replied that while the endpoint had to be precise, en route the module was continually drifting a degree or two off course.

The key was continually correcting that course.

We humans are blessed with the most sophisticated guidance system ever created. It's not about always being right, it's about continual course correction, and because our innate system is always working on that, we can relax and enjoy the ride.

A colleague in India shared with me something so true it knocked me sideways.

She's a team lead and had asked her husband - someone with many years' experience leading large and diverse teams - how to prevent problems from arising.

He responded with the following:

"When someone is hooked to an ECG and it flat lines, it means that person is dead. A fluctuating ECG means the person is alive."

To put it another way, problems are a sign of life.

They are perfectly natural. Normal.

Problems are only what we make of them.

Some things we view as a problem may be a breeze to someone else.

Problems which are intractable to others we might barely think about.

Something which is a huge problem to us one day can be simple the next day, without any change in circumstance.

There is no intrinsic value in any experience.

Like our ECG, thoughts and experience fluctuate moment to moment.

Not good, not bad, just signs of life, and the less it looks to us as though problems are coming from something other than Thought, the less problematic our lives will be.

A thought is a spark which can ignite a fire.

One time I learned a trusted work friend had complained about my handling of a project to the boss of my boss.

He had never mentioned any misgivings as we were working, but now I learnt that he felt out of the loop, that things were disorganized and his team had not been engaged in the right way.

I quickly became angry. To my mind, I had communicated frequently, provided multiple options for interaction between teams and made it clear that if he, or any of his staff had doubts or questions, they only had to ask.

They had simply chosen not to take me up on those options.

That was their problem!

I didn't see it, but I had fanned an initial spark and started a fire.

The more our team discussed the situation, the more outraged we became.

We had moved heaven and earth to anticipate their every whim, and not only were they being difficult and unresponsive, they now had the gall to make us look bad to our bosses and pretend the options we had given had never been offered.

We talked about being less open with this individual.

Of copying our bosses into our communications, so they could see where the problem really lay, of reporting this individual's divisive behaviour as a risk to the success of the project.

We had now poured gasoline onto the burgeoning flames and created a raging inferno.

I left that team meeting full of righteous indignation.

But when quietly reflecting on the events, it occurred to me that the person in question was a long-time friend and that such behaviour was very out of character.

That he might be feeling stressed in his new job, that maybe he was just protecting his own back.

I also had not heard his perspective from his own lips, but from team mates in a highly charged emotional state.

And that they had heard these stories from our boss.

Who had heard them from his boss.

Before I heard these stories, they had been interpreted by the filters and perspectives of at least three different people.

I wondered if the intent of my friend was not what I heard, that his perspective was different.

Maybe his view of the world differed from that of my boss, his boss and my team mates.

Maybe it was different from my view of the world.

Then it occurred to me to wonder where exactly the fire was.

The answer came - in my own head.

Nowhere else.

When we blame our feelings on something other than Thought, it is like trying to put out the flames engulfing your own house by throwing water on next door.

As I realized the scenario was all my own creation, the flames began to subside.

I was intact, unburnt and knew what to do - to go meet with my friend and get a better understanding of his view of the situation and find out what could have been done differently.

Now all I wanted to do was listen, to really get his world.

As we talked, my feeling of warmth for him returned.

It was a simple misunderstanding.

We had both made assumptions as to what the other was thinking and intending.

The feeling was such that I could gently share what a furore his email to my boss's boss had created - for which, he was most apologetic.

It had never been his intent to create bad feeling, he simply wanted clarity.

A thought is nothing more than a spark, it is we who tend to it and choose to fan it into a flame, or let it die.

The infernos, should they come, are never happening anywhere other than in our own home.

We will forget that, a hundred times or more every day.

But whenever we remember where the fires truly originate, the immediate neighbourhood is saved from being consumed by flames and we can return to living peacefully in the gentle warmth of Thought.

126

I was once at Universal Studios in Florida, a magical theme park with rides which excite, beguile and enchant.

I had just finished Skull Island. The truck in which I was riding had been battered, rocked and plunged into a ravine as a Tyrannosaurus Rex tried to make us his breakfast. We were only saved from certain death by the timely intervention of Kong, who swung in and beat the marauders back.

An exhilarating, adrenaline fuelled experience.

Except it didn't quite happen like that.

We were actually sitting in a vehicle which was being rocked and shaken, as the images of the attack were projected by surrounding screens and enhanced by various special effects like water, wind sprays and the virtual reality goggles we were wearing.

We were perfectly safe.

My reactions were generated in exactly the same way as they are in any other moment - by Thought taking all the data available and creating a simulation which then appeared to me as reality.

Our use of Thought makes some situations seem more real than others.

For instance, since learning about where my experience is really coming from, I am less scared of rollercoaster simulators, because I know they are much more stationary than they feel - that the sudden accelerations, decelerations, sharp ascents and plunges, are cleverly created illusions.

Because I have an embodied understanding of how things work, I can enjoy the ride and appreciate the creativity which created it, rather than being scared.

Now, outdoor rollercoasters plunge and rise, accelerate, twist and turn, doing so along a very visible and real track which quite often appears to defy gravity.

I intellectually understand my experience of those is also a projection of Thought.

But I can't get on them. I'm scared stiff.

I don't truly believe my experience would be 100%

Thought generated.

It really seems as though the rollercoaster would have something to do with it.

But that's ok.

We will always have blind spots where we believe influences other than Thought are in play. That's what being human is all about.

As our understanding of how life really works gets ever deeper, so these blind spots are revealed, and when they are, we are better able to enjoy whatever experience Thought is simulating in that moment, no matter what it might be.

.

127

In the early part of 2016, my mother's health began to deteriorate rapidly. There had already been a gradual decline in her independence, mobility and ability to do things for herself. Now she was weak and frail, unable to walk unaided, anxious, frightened and completely reliant on my brother – her chief care giver – for everything.

Concerned that her death might be imminent, that she needed better care than he could provide, my brother asked that I visit urgently, so we might look after her together while deciding what the best course of action might be.

The day after I arrived my brother was hospitalized with a collapsed lung, leaving me alone to care for mum.

After a momentary panic, a deep feeling of peace and calm descended on me. I stayed in the present moment. I did things I would never have dreamt of doing, nor would have wanted to. But I felt no pressure to do anything other than what needed to be done. There was no worry about the future. I was in this place for nearly two weeks, and while occasionally I would drop out of it, I would always be reminded of the space within me which would provide what I needed.

We moved mum to a residential home, where she stayed for the last three weeks of her life until she passed.

I experienced much peace in her final days, because I deeply felt that her ailment was only a physical one which could not touch her true essence; the spirit within which existed long before taking my mother's form and would exist long after leaving it.

It was as though her spirit felt her physical form no longer worked, and it was time to move on.

The experience made me realize anew the amazing capacity of the human system to provide what we need when we need it. I didn't have to have distraught, confused feelings about the situation. Whatever we are experiencing, it can and will change, naturally. We get in trouble not because of our thoughts and feelings, but because of what we make of those - our all too human tendency to believe things should be a certain way.

We are the sky and our thoughts but passing weather - the sky has no opinion about the weather, it merely allows it to pass through. Sunshine or thunderstorms are not good or bad, they just are.

As for mum, well, she's out there somewhere, and, as in life, will always live in my thoughts.

To paraphrase Billy Crystal in his incredibly moving eulogy for his friend Muhammad Ali,

"She is gone, but she will never die."

128

One of the enthusiasms I inherited from my dear mum was a love for the 1950s BBC radio show, The Goons.

It was ridiculous, uproariously funny and quite often would be concluded by the announcer solemnly saying,

"It's all in the mind, you know".

One time, our heroes were trudging through the desert, tired and desperately hungry.

One of them, Seagoon, sees a house in the distance. Colonel Bloodnok insists it's a mirage but still they rush to investigate and the listeners are treated to the sounds of doors banging and hurried footsteps as they explore.

But then Seagoon laments,

"You were right, it was a mirage"

as the house fades.

Suddenly a yell and a loud bang is heard as Eccles crashes to the floor.

Bloodnok asks,

"Eccles, what happened?"

To which Eccles replies,

"I was upstairs!"

The story is ludicrous and funny.

We don't take it seriously, because it is so obviously made up.

But it's interesting how our perception of what is made up, and what's not made up, can fluctuate so wildly from person to person, and even within the same person from moment to moment.

Your wife is late home, so there must have been a car accident.

I didn't answer that question very well - so I've blown the interview.

Because in that moment the scenario looks plausible, we buy into it.

But the truth of it, no matter what the situation, is always the same:

"It's all in the mind, you know."

EPILOGUE

Some learning how experience is only ever a momentary reflection of Thought rather than circumstances might object,

"But what about extreme cases, such as being the victim of a crime like domestic abuse?

Are you saying that did not have a real impact?

Are you saying the events will not influence the future of that person?

That they will not have scars?"

No.

These principles don't deny human experience, they are simply an explanation of how it works.

Whether you are happy or suffering, whether you have been the victim of a crime or not, the human experience only works one way for everyone, although often we will be convinced otherwise.

While it may not look like it, our suffering is only ever created by us believing it is coming from somewhere other than Thought.

As we move through life, we build in our minds a cityscape of how the world works.

The buildings are constructed from our hopes, fears, our likes, dislikes and so on.

The more we believe in the objective reality of our experiences, the more we reinforce the buildings in our mind, the more they become skyscrapers and the busier the city becomes with construction work.

Those who suffer the most feel trapped by the buildings, struggling for air or to glimpse the sky between these monstrous edifices.

But as knowledge of how experience is being created becomes more embodied within us, so the bricks and walls of these buildings begin to crumble.

Over time, the buildings start to collapse, often taking others with them.

It works the same for any human being, irrespective of

their health or life history - the more the true source of experience is recognised, the more the landscape clears.

We will always be constructing some building or other.

But when you know the true nature of the landscape is to be clear - that at any moment we can demolish what we have created and start anew —

There is so much hope in that.

For everyone.

ACKNOWLEDGMENTS

To all the wonderful practitioners in this community for the writings, workshops and calls that have both impacted and inspired me, including:

Sydney Banks, Michael Neill, George and Linda Pransky, Barb Patterson, Elsie Spittle, Jan and Chip Chipman, Dr Bill Pettit, Jonny Bowden, Mamoon Yusaf, Dr Keith Blevens, Valda Monroe, Sandy Krot, Dr Ken Manning and Robin Charbit.

To the community of Clarity Coaches for their love, friendship, wisdom and support.

To the following dear friends:

Adam Ashe, Dr Ken Manning, Elissa Clash, Simon Christopher, Neil Root, Phil White, Cris Hay, Clesia Mendes and Chemeckia Banks - for kindly offered feedback and encouragement on rough drafts.

Lesly Bohuchot, for her suggestions on book cover colour combinations.

Dr Aaron Turner, for his mentoring during the One Thought programme and for introducing me to the power of listening without judgement.

Jamie Smart, for his guidance during the Clarity Coach programme, for the challenge to take action - which led to the metaphors you have read in this book - and for helping me to see the profound difference between the power of Thought and thinking.

Dr Amy Johnson, for her foreword, encouragement and countless conversations which have taken me ever deeper in this understanding.

Garret Kramer, for his time, guidance and the book which was the catalyst that changed my life forever.

Bonnie Jarvis, for crafting the awesome book cover design, website and animations that accompany this book. Many thanks also to StockUnlimited, for usage of the globe image in the cover design.

Andrew Cobble, ex co-worker and now writer and publisher for helping me get this book out into the world.

And to my family - my brother, my outlaws and my beautiful and amazing wife and daughters – Debbie, Lulu and Lexie – words can never express how much I love you all, how grateful I am for your love and for being able to share this wonderful life with you.

And last, but by no means least, my thanks to you, the reader. If even one of the metaphors in these pages has given you pause for thought, this book has done its job.

My love and deepest gratitude to you all.

I can't wait to see where the journey takes us next.

FURTHER EXPLORATIONS

If you are interested in deepening your understanding of the human experience and the innate well-being which is the birthright of everyone in this world, I'd love to help. I offer personal coaching in ways that can be tailored to your needs.

Please contact me at:

Email: philanthonyhughes@gmail.com

Facebook: phil.hughes.3785

Website: itsallinthemindyouknow.com

Below is a selection of the books which have had a big impact on me:

The Missing Link by Sydney Banks (Lone Pine Publishing, 1998)

The Enlightened Gardener by Sydney Banks (Lone Pine Publishing, 2001)

The Enlightened Gardener Revisited by Sydney Banks (Lone Pine Publishing, 2005)

Stillpower by Garret Kramer (Simon & Schuster, 2012)

The Path of No Resistance by Garret Kramer (Greenleaf Book Group, 2015)

Clarity by Jamie Smart (Wiley, 2013)

The Little Book of Clarity by Jamie Smart (Capstone, 2015)

Results by Jamie Smart (Capstone, 2016)

The Little Book of Results by Jamie Smart (Capstone, 2018)

Invisible Power by Ken Manning, Robin Charbit and Sandy Krot (Insight Principles, 2015)

Being Human by Dr Amy Johnson (Amy Johnson, 2013)

The Little Book of Big Change by Dr Amy Johnson (New Harbinger, 2016)

The Inside-Out Revolution by Michael Neill (Hay House, 2013)

The Space Within by Michael Neill (Hay House, 2016)

Creating the Impossible by Michael Neill (Hay House, 2018)

Coming Home by Dicken Bettinger and Natasha Swerdloff (CreateSpace, 2016)

Just Play by Nick Bottini (Rethink Press, 2018)

Beyond Imagination by Elsie Spittle (CreateSpace, 2013)

Nuggets of Wisdom by Elsie Spittle (CreateSpace, 2016)

The Relationship Handbook by George Pransky (Pransky & Associates, 2017)

Somebody Should Have Told Us by Jack Pransky (CCB Publishing, 2011)

ABOUT THE AUTHOR

Phil Hughes is forty-seven years old but by the time you read this may be older. He lives in Sunningdale in England with his beautiful wife and two daughters who claim to be thirteen and eleven, but he doesn't believe this for a moment. They also have a cat who is forever hungry no matter how much food we put in her bowl.

This is his first published work.

34177521R00141

Made in the USA
Middletown, DE
23 January 2019